And a
Nightingale Sang

By Marianne Sells
Collated by Claire Sells

DEDICATION

Dedicated to my mother's memory and sisters,
Diana and Cynthia.

CONTENTS

ACKNOWLEDGEMENTS

With very special thanks to:
Nicola Kaufmann, Lynn Futter, Marilyn Curzon,
Rachel Hibberd, Autumn House staff, Holly at Beiersdorf
(Nivea) UK and Ireland, Wyn at Kilner and Aaron Williams

1 IT'S WAR!

In the summer of 1939, it was hot and balmy as each day folded gently into another. We (I was the seventh of a family of ten plus my parents, two brothers, Gregory and Eric, and several sisters; June, Gay, Felicity, Diana, Patricia, Elaine and Kathy) lived in Hayling Island, near Portsmouth. Our house, "White Lodge," was a rambling one - white with a green-tiled roof, Mediterranean in style, with pinks growing in cracks from the grey, crazy paving drive that stretched to the house and garage. It was here that my father ran his dental practice. He had set it up on his own, purchasing the equipment (dental chair, instruments etc.) at his own expense and at great cost. I vividly remember the chair and bureaus of small drawers filled with dental floss samples. The temptation of such delights was often too much, my sisters and I used to sneak in and sample all the different products when we thought no one was looking, taking turns to move each other up and down in the dental chair.

My father found it a struggle, as there was no NHS then and often patients could not or would not pay him. Unfortunately due to this and the largeness of the family as well as him being too kind-hearted, we owed shopkeepers and lived in poverty most of the time. Despite this he was a very good dental surgeon and the dental plates he made for patients were excellent and lasted for ages. He trained at Guys Hospital and The Royal Dental Hospital, just like his father.

Every day that summer, the sun lit up our house and Daddy, looking very dapper in his short, white coat, tended to his patients. Sometimes we heard children yelling and I remember seeing a trail of blood up the path from the surgery, after a tooth extraction. Hardly confidence inspiring for us children, whom Daddy treated too! I remember being chased around the dental chair, hotly pursued by him, my mouth clamped shut in fear!

The little drawers of medical samples were an endless fascination, but an angry roar from my father soon made us run into the garden. Here a cherry tree grew, and fat, red peonies drooped onto the paths, but woe betide any of us whom ventured to the end of the garden because there lived Daddy's bantams, his pride and joy. The males would come flying out to attack anyone daring to venture into their territory, and we were really afraid of their sharp beaks.

The house was also supposed to be haunted, apparently by a departed servant girl who would get up early in the morning and go downstairs. Her footsteps could be heard by several members of my family but not by me. I was sent upstairs by my father to his workroom, the passage leading up to it was in darkness apart from a stream of light across it. The door to the room was open but I was literally frozen to the floor in fear. After a while I was able to crawl downstairs but I had never felt so frightened as I did then.

At the back of the house there was a big field where once a day a tractor delivered swedes and various produce to the cows who grazed there. My older sister (by a year and a half) would drag me through a hole in the fence and run off when the cows were let out after milking. My short little legs couldn't run as fast so I was left surrounded by giant cows eating the vegetables with enormous tongues. I was terrified and convinced that they were going to eat me!

Sometimes the family would hoist me up on the high wall at the end of the garden to beg the postman for black cherries and sweets. Of course I didn't get a chance to eat these goodies as I had to distribute them to the others waiting below!

All my sisters' friends were large and leggy, so it seemed they would either drop something on me or fall on me. Rubber tyres swinging from trees on ropes would wind me. When they raided my father's strawberry patch, I was unable to run away fast enough and would be met with a sharp smack on the bottom from my father's cane carpet beater as he angrily bellowed at me!

There was also a running feud with the Jehovah Witness family that lived next to us. Tales of deprivation and beatings were regularly told by two pale faced and bespectacled, pig tailed little girls. However, they always seemed clean and scrubbed in appearance. We never found out whether they were telling the truth or not, but I felt sorry for them.

Further along the coast, my grandfather, Sir Richard Gregory, Bart, FRS, lived. He was a great visionary and was a man before his times. (More details can be found about him on the internet, under the title "Sir Richard Gregory – His Life and Times.") His wife was Kate Florence, my mother's mother. She suffered badly from arthritis and was confined to a wheelchair – so much so that my mother needed to be near her, as her health was so poor.

Grandfather's house was large, well staffed with servants and overlooked the sand dunes and the sea. Grandfather led a busy life as editor of "Nature" and Pathé News. He warned the world of the danger of the nuclear bomb. He was also a good friend of H.G. Wells, George Bernard Shaw and Marie Stopes and he wrote many books. Grandfather was very worried about the fact that there so many mouths to feed, and sometimes he would turn out with food baskets for us and Grandmother would bring blankets, as the Depression was biting and a lot of poverty lay underneath the veneer of wealth.

With the exception of our grandparents, our family members looked down at us, the terrible unwieldy Fowlers! In fact, if it had been the seventies we might have been a social worker's dream!

Despite all the problems, we were basically a happy family and my parents were very much in love. My mother trained at the Royal Academy of Music and was a professional pianist and violinist. She had trained with Myra Hess and played with the Royal Philharmonic Orchestra. There was always a piano in the house, which she played frequently, playing many works, such as "Fingal's Cave", all through with no music sheets. I also remember her playing the violin, sitting on the edge of her bed, at her father's house, also at Walberton, Sussex, while I played on the floor as a small girl of about three years.

One of my mother's dearest friends was a school teacher's daughter, we used to climb up their wall and call 'Can we come over?' If the answer was yes, the school master used to put a ladder up for us to climb down and then invite us in for Beatrix Potter stories and delicious spongefingers. Usually accompanied by clear, cool lemonade in long glasses.

When the war was declared, I was six years and eight months, and not due to go to school until I was seven, which was the expected age at that time.

We never expected a war, and so life went on more or less as normal, with summer days spent on the beach, where my brothers and sisters were cared for either by a batty old Nanny called "Mary" or a friend of my mother, Nurse Coates. Sometimes we were also taken out by the elder sisters, usually June, Elaine or Patricia (although I must add that on the odd occasion it did end in disaster!)

We dug for shells and crabs in rock pools and paddled in the sea.

One of Nurse Coates' sons had a birthday party, and sandwiches and an iced cake were handed around, the latter attracting many wasps – we all screamed! The smell of the sea and hot sand were sleep inducing and in the sun's haze the curve of the beach seemed to go on forever, to the end of the world.

A man pushing a small cart sold penny ices and the crunch of the feet on the pebbles meant the crab seller was on his way - a young lad with a basket slung over his shoulders, in which lay orange-cooked crabs.

As the sun began to dip behind the sea, it was time to return home and bedtime. Time to say "Goodnight" to my mother and father and to go to bed in the large bedroom at the top of the house, with picture windows that looked out to the ocean.

Some days my mother would take me to look from her bedroom window at the Queen Mary gliding up the Solent on her way out of Southampton, and with all her lights ablaze at night. I would always dream of the glamorous life onboard her.

All felt right with the world, but dark forces were gathering and Pandora was to open the box and unleash terrible evils, which even to this day, continue to haunt the world, and these evil deeds would alter all our lives, forever.

In late summer, war was declared and my father joined the Royal Army Medical Corps, RAMC, his regiment was the Royal Ulster Rifles. His rank was Captain, later to be Major. He wore a hat with a green cockade and he was stationed in Bally Kinlar Camp, Northern Ireland, and at Blackpool.

When my father was gone we had to move away to what we thought was a safer area, away from the coast, as Portsmouth was being bombed. The brave people at Hayling were lighting beacons on the beaches to draw the fire away from the docks in an attempt to save our ships.

My parents hired a taxi and drove into Sussex to look for a safer place and house, and they found an old farmhouse called "Snapelands" in a village called Lodsworth. It was there that we were to stay for the duration of the war, which we thought would last for a year or two, but of course lasted for six years and was to disrupt our lives forever.

Now that we had arranged to move, we had to find a removal van, an almost impossible task, as Pickfords and all other forms of transport had gone for moving troops and the war effort.

At last a cattle truck was found and we, as well as our furniture, were hastily put on board. There were stray bits of straw on the floor and a strong, unpleasant smell of manure. Mother travelled in a taxi at the front with our youngest sister, Felicity, then only a year old and very fretful. We remained under the watchful eye of our eldest sister, Cynthia, as we bumped along the winding roads of Sussex.

In a sense, we were refugees, displaced and fleeing for our lives, like so many in Europe, never to see their homes again even to this day. As the lorry swayed along, a stone jar fell on my sister Gay's head and she started to cry. My head was full of questions: Where in the world were we going? Why was our old life gone? In fact it was to be changed forever and after the war, nothing would be left but hardship and debris. We eventually managed to traverse the village road and a rough farm track to Snapelands (a different name for 'snipe', which was a local bird in great abundance at the time).

The Sussex farmhouse that nestled in the valley seemed to be a safe haven. It was to hold our hopes and fears for the oncoming war and we prayed our new dwelling would ensure our survival.

A day after we left Hayling Island, a bomb fell on the

house next door and burned it to the ground, we were lucky to have moved just in time.

2 LIFE AT SNAPELANDS

Snapelands was a typical Sussex farmhouse built in the 11th or 12th century in Lodsworth (situated between Midhurst and Petworth). It was very damp, with rough distemper walls, in soft colours of pale peach and white. It was very primitive – there was no electricity, a soak away for drainage and water from a fresh spring was piped into the house. Forget central heating, there was only a black, all-purpose stove for heating and cooking on, which my sister Gay frequently polished with black lead.

The small village where we were based was self-sufficient, with a village store, separate post office, (with an old-fashioned counter), vet, shoemakers, blacksmiths and two women who laundered. Two doctors also resided in nearby Midhurst, who would come out for a fee if one was ill. There was also the village bobby on a bicycle who would put the fear of God into little boys who misbehaved!

Mother had a coal fire in the sitting room and this was her private room, although Daddy would sit there all night when he was on leave (which was seldom during the war). Her room was also a place where we could listen to the BBC Children's Hour on the radio. We had to sit very still and listen whilst seated at a round table made of mahogany.

We would often sit around the big, scrubbed kitchen

table by the warm kitchen range and played various games such as Snap, Ludo and Snakes and Ladders. My brother Gregory would cry if he didn't win! In the middle of the table was an oil lamp, casting a warm glow on our faces and we would drink cocoa that Cynthia made before bedtime. It was here that we felt safest and forgot about our worries and the war. The kitchen range glowed, it was rather hot in the summer but we had to keep it on as it was our only means of cooking and heating water. Sometimes the odd pot simmered on the stove, full of potato peelings and scraps, to be fed to our hens later.

I loved the scrubbed table on which we also ate our meals. When Daddy was home, my parents would sit at both ends and when he was away, my mother alone at one end.

After living in centrally heated houses, the cold of the farmhouse that chilled our bones was a great shock! As it was so dreadful we wore vests that were tremendously itchy, liberty bodices which were like waistcoats and buttoned over our vests, to keep warm. Sometimes we even wore thick combinations, an all-in-one garment with a flap for convenience! We also had tick knickers for underwear and on top thick jumpers, balaclavas on our heads (with just our eyes showing), cosy socks and woollen gloves.

One of my sisters said that the house was like "Cold, Comfort Farm" in the winter! At night it was so unbearably cool that we would put our overcoats and old grey army blankets over our beds and use a stone hot water bottle or brick warmed in the oven and wrapped in an old scarf or jumper for our frozen toes. Our cat would often join us too, one morning I was woken up by an assortment of meows as her kittens came into the world! Strangely we did not have as many colds and coughs as we seem to today and no fleas on the animals!

Once I put myself to bed with all my clothes on and the next day my school uniform was all crumpled up. My teacher Miss Osbourne on seeing me said, "Marianne, you look like you've been pulled through a hedge backwards!." Little did she know!

I shared my bedroom in a large room with three of my sisters, Gay, Elaine and Diana, and sometimes we would snuggle together for warmth. The wind howled around the house, snatching at the stones and whining in frustration. In the morning the house felt even colder with damp, clammy walls, and we found it even harder to get out of our warm beds and get changed in the room. But downstairs in the warm kitchen the black range was brought to life by Cynthia and the kettle and porridge made ready for breakfast. Steaming mugs of tea were very welcome. It was very hard for Cynthia as she was doing a strenuous job, she was very clever and loved local history, but all the help in the house had gone to the munitions factory, army or to nursing, so my sister had to look after us instead. She coped admirably, but was very strict and doled out hard smacks! She also did all the washing up, got us up for school and did the housework. Mrs. Wakeford, a local cottager, came occasionally to scrub the kitchen and scullery floors and do other bits when needed.

My mother would consume her breakfast in bed and usually arose at eleven in the morning, to have her hot chocolate and prepare lunch. She had taken a cordon bleu course and was a superb cook. Apart from the cooking, she led very much a lady's life, which meant she never did housework or gardened, or did any kind of physical work. At her grandfather's house, she shared a ladies' maid with her mother, who did her hair, brought her tea in the mornings and drew the curtains. It must have been harder now with my father at war and the care required by such a big family.

She was very clever at languages, speaking German and French, as did my father, and had attended Chichester High School and then the Royal Academy of Music. She had not experienced any real hardship in her life (apart from her mother's ill health) but of course all that changed with the advent of the war and my father absent.

Sometimes my mind would return to "White Lodge" and once again I pictured my parents dancing to their wind-up gramophone, my father, slim, blonde and dapper, my mother - small and dark. I would often reminisce of our ordered life there, which seemed like the Hamptons of New York, our gracious 1930s house with its lovely rooms, décor and furniture. I enjoyed the social whirl of our aunts and uncles and various other friends and relatives visiting us in their grand cars. Now this close-knit circle was to be scattered far and wide and bonds were to be broken.

At night when mother came to kiss me goodnight and I smelt her violet perfume, I would always feel a sense of happiness. Her great affection for her children was always apparent, even though this was a time when society expected you not to interact with your offspring. Mother tried her best with all of us but it was a mammoth task due to there being so many children. I remember my third birthday I had a white iced cake with violets on. Mother found it hard to give attention to each of us as she sat opposite her friend from across a low table. Now here at Snapelands the old days had gone and we faced a spartan life. Mother would cook the lunch and after we were all fed, retire to her sitting room with a cup of tea whilst reading The Telegraph with the radio on in the background. It was a daunting task for my mother as my father would be away travelling around the country, stationed in various places such as Surrey, Blackpool and Northern Ireland. He was barely in contact with us and travelled in blacked out trains, only to announce his arrival home by tapping on the window (usually late at night). We would always rush to greet him as he came into the kitchen. We had to be very discreet as "Careless Talk Cost Lives" posters would advise us. He never wrote or telephoned as it was deemed too dangerous.

Once Daddy said that whilst crossing the Irish Sea, his ship had been chased by a German submarine, which came out of Southern Ireland where the Germans were. In order to lose them, the Captain had 'zig-zagged' the ship all the way – Daddy said it was very exciting! In the winter when Daddy was on leave, he would sit with Mother at the coal fire in the sitting room, content reading the paper and our dog at his feet.

We were alone in the isolated farmhouse, there were no streetlights or friendly neighbours. In the summer, the owls called in the twilight and the smell of roses and jasmine floated on the warm air, with the occasional call of a fox.

I was afraid at night as it was so dark, so to comfort us Mother would put a torch under our pillows, but we could never find it or it had fallen down! We did not like calling for help as we did not want to disturb our parents, the little time they had together was so precious. Those were the days that children respected their parents and looked up to them, and wouldn't march into the sitting room at night without knocking on the door.

Now that Daddy was away, the house revolved around my mother and her word was law! As the days went by we began to adapt to life in the country and the roughness of our new life. We would hear the unfamiliar sounds of the country - birds, tractors, cows and other animals and general rural life around us.

However, despite all the hardships, I began to be fascinated by the new world around me and the beautiful countryside, I gradually fell in love with my new surroundings and continue to have a keen fondness for unspoilt and serene land.

3 FARMING LIFE (OF HARVEST TIME, HEAVY HORSES AND CREATURES)

We had inherited a working farm when we moved to Snapelands, which my second eldest sister, June, was to run. She was now officially a land girl and wore the uniform of khaki dungarees, short sleeved cotton shirts, thick green jumpers, a short khaki coat in the winter, Wellingtons and sometimes jodhpurs.

June had a private education and was a 'young lady', and we were all eventually due to attend Queen Charlotte's Ball for our coming out as debutantes. We were in Debrett's and Who's Who, but all was to be overtaken by the urgency of war and a dream my parents had cherished was no more.

Poor June was out in all weathers. She had to learn to milk the cows (of which there were about six to eight) by hand, drive the tractor, cut the hedges and dig the ditches. I remember that her Wellington boots were often caked in Sussex clay. The fields had to be weeded by hand as there wasn't weed killer then! We were particularly precious about ridding the land of ragwort, deceptively pretty yellow flowers but deadly to cows and horses. Not one weed was allowed to flourish. I did notice however, that it was often covered in black and yellow striped caterpillars, but I never see these now. Funnily enough though, I still see lots of ragwort in the present day which surprises me knowing how lethal it can be to livestock.

I did my bit on the farm too, mucking out the cowshed and washing it down, plus feeding the calves with buckets of milk. I loved the way that they sucked up the milk through my fingers – their big, heavy lashed eyes reminded me of Hollywood film stars!

Gay was very good with the calves and loved feeding them too. June had to get up very early to milk the cows, even in the coldest winter. She was my second eldest sister and only in her teens so she had a very hard job to maintain. The farmers that remained on the land helped her the best they could, most of them were too young or old to be in active service. The work on the land was very important and we should not forget that they saved the country from starvation. Getting food into this country was almost impossible and we were reliant on the farmers and their efforts. Many farmers are not valued now as they once were, but they were essential to us during the war. Their day will surely I hope come again.

George, who was based at Redlands Farm just over the hill from us, would plough the fields with the one remaining tractor. When the crops were ready to be harvested, the farmer from the next village would inspect the golden, rustling fields and then roll a piece of corn between his fingers. He would then bite it between his teeth, and if it was ready to be harvested it was time to start long days in the hot summer fields, hard but rewarding work.

Harvest time was much more enjoyable and fulfilling then, the fields a beautiful shade of orange. Whole families were always involved and summer holidays where the children were free enabled them to help out. When it was time to harvest I couldn't wait until the end of school! I loved that time, spending all day assisting with the harvest and gathering it in with the farm workers.

Sometimes it would be me that would lead the carthorse

through the fields to pick up the stooks of corn. I was very careful to do it properly so I wouldn't be shouted at! The stooks were stacked several together, the men tied them with string which they kept in their pockets (the ends always visibly trailing down) and cut with a knife. The heavy horses were magnificent creatures and I adored them, we didn't have much petrol then so relied on them for transport. Before the war, often the big horses were adorned with brasses and wore their tails in plaits, there were some magnificent ones that were owned by Lord Cowdray and the accompanying carts were painted yellow. Some farms had a Carter whose job was solely to look after the horses, he kept them beautifully and groomed them so well that their coats gleamed. In fact, one of the most amusing sights was to see them put out to grass in the summer. Their hooves would thunder as they playfully chased each other across the fields, kicking up their hooves in the most ridiculous manner, their loud neighs punctuating the air. These lovely creatures had such personalities that it was sad to see so many put down after the war, until there were almost none left. But once again they are becoming popular and in some cases replacing the tractor. I always associate horses with farming, in my mind, the two are inseparable, there is always something beautiful about a field with horses in, like a moving landscape. It seems to me that men and animals need each other, one appears to complement the other.

There was not much of a childhood for us then, you were just another pair of hands. Certainly no such thing as a teenager with their own culture. We were little old people trapped in children's bodies.

At noon the farmhand's wife would bring a napkin-covered basket, which contained bread, farmhouse cheese, fruitcake and iced cold tea (the drink having been lowered into the well to cool).

I was supposed to go home but liked to stay out. In the

shade of the great old oak tree, we would share the meal. The chilled tea was served from an earthenware jug and was like nectar to our parched throats, the bread was so fresh, the fruitcake deliciously moist and crumbly. There was also cider and egg pie. All around we would hear the soft lilt of Sussex voices. Some of the men would stretch out and snooze in the warmth of the day. There were always people in the fields as well as the cows, sheep and horses. Everything was made use of and nothing went to waste. The old Sussex families worked the land, the weft and weave of old customs, written through them like rock.

When the harvest was almost over, the fields were full of stubble and an occasional pheasant strutted about, gleaning the leftover pieces of corn, and busy field mice and dormice scurried around. This was the field that George had ploughed well into dusk as our efforts were very much needed.

Once he stopped the tractor and carefully lifted the ploughshare over a plover's nest and eggs. The mother flew off but thankfully returned later. We used to call these birds 'Peewits' as this was their call. We found the sound soothing as they swooped over the land.

During the war we had a great loyalty to each other as well as the land and we gave as much as we could without ever counting the cost.

At the culmination of the harvest the threshing machine arrived and would work tirelessly until all the corn was bagged up and ready to be used. We relied on our farms to feed us and became very adept at self-sufficiency.

On this hot summer's day as the sun beat down, the smell of the heat, dust from the thresher and oil from the machines was very potent. Sometimes the odd rat would rush out from the loads of corn and be swiftly dispatched by the men.

Soon there would be a harvest festival in St. Peter's, the little church, golden ears of corn in a sheaf and various fruits and vegetables surrounding the altar. Many women bottled the produce from their gardens or hedgerows in Kilner jars and made jams, chutney and pickles. Apples were stored in the loft, carrots and potatoes in outhouses and even hen eggs stored in a special solution.

I was very lucky to have helped in the harvest and seen the whole process from the first sowing of the seeds in the glad earth, which had been tilled for hundreds of years and only natural manure used, so it was organic.

Now a huge harvest moon climbed high in the evening sky and the white ghost of a barn owl glided silently past me. The fruits of the earth had been gathered in, the earth would sleep again until it awakened the following spring.

It was at such times that we could almost forget about the unhappiness of the war, for a short time at least. Although, not dissimilar to a fretful child, we would soon be sharply reminded as events of the war returned to haunt us.

For now, the Church of St. Peter stands with the monkey-puzzle tree at the gate and grey-green graves. Many old families sleep here. The river flows through the fields, all is peaceful and serene. From the woods the nightjar calls whilst twilight falls softly.

The days of the long summer rolled by and one season inevitably followed another, each one though was as important as the next and to be savoured. The hay meadow was cut and when the working day had ended, it was loaded into a cart to be moved to Redlands Farm. I clambered on top with George's brother, Peter, for my first hayride. As the tractor bumped along I reflected on what a lovely trip it was – we worked so hard that this was one of the perks on the job!

4 THE BATTLE FOR BRITAIN

When the Battle of Britain started in the late summer of 1940 it felt at times as if it was taking place over the farm! Planes swooped and swung over the land and above our heads engaging in "dog fights", firing at one another. The greatest air battle of the war had begun and was to prove one of the most decisive battles of the Second World War as it was to turn the tide in our country's favour. We would have lost the war without these brave pilots and the sacrifices they made for us. There were so many young men dying in their prime.

At night my brothers and sisters and I lay in bed listening to the thrum of the Lancaster bombers going over our heads in large numbers, sometimes only the black silhouettes of the planes could be seen against the clear night skies. At least an hour would go by as thousands of planes were flying over for intensive bombing raids and I would fall asleep. The Merlin engines sounded determined and steadfast just like the men flying them, so we felt comforted and safe. If it was a full moon it was much better to bomb by as the targets were clearly visible. But of course not safe for the crews, who were very vulnerable to the enemy in the moonlight (they also faced terrible obstacles apart from this, such as barrage balloons and guns). We always knew that when the moon was at this phase the magnificent Lancasters would fly.

During the day, stray German fighters flew over and would fire guns at children and women on the ground. I don't know if they came from France or Germany, but they always came alone, dropping stray bombs before returning to their bases.

There was also to be another enemy terror which was to come and Mother was unable to shield us. The buzz bombs – the bomb that travelled alone and was not dropped, this bomb would be the forerunner to the rocket and was terrifying. It would be set to drop on specific targets. Fortunately out of our range, but rather a hit or miss affair. The noise that they made was distant, a rather rough noise, which would sputter intermittently. We would watch them pass over – first a red flame followed by billowing clouds of black smoke. We narrowly missed one once, hearing it overhead we immediately flung ourselves to the ground, only for it to carry on a few more miles before plummeting and creating a huge crater, fortunately not leaving any other damage.

Sniping was a regular occurrence and once Cynthia was in the woods with Gay when suddenly the earth started flying up as a German was firing at them, so they dove into the nearest ditch. The terror came from the skies and this made us feel apprehensive, we began to fear the open fields and took to the woods, where hidden from view we felt safer amongst the thick trees.

Once my brother Gregory and I were in the field nearest the house and a fighter plane came low over the fields. My mother and June were in the top bedroom and on seeing the plane, June waved a tea towel out the window whilst shouting "Good old Britain!" We saw the swastikas on the wings shining in the sunlight and fear suddenly rooted us to the spot, Gregory grabbed my hand and we started running. I looked up above us as the plane seemed to slow down and hover, the helmeted head peered down at us, guns primed and ready. Mother shouted with great presence of mind "Lie down!" We flung ourselves on the dried earth and out of the corner of my eye, I saw him staring down, then he swooped over the house and was gone. We had not been shot which was unusual, that pilot saved our lives as we were easy targets. In that moment he had shown compassion, perhaps he had children of his own?

I understand that a cow was shot on another farm at Arundel, only a few miles away. A poor unfortunate little boy aged only six was machine gunned at Amberley in Sussex, as he jumped into a ditch with Ron, another boy, both evacuees from London. A different pilot I hope. A school in the next village (Petworth) was completely destroyed and all 30 children were killed. Mum was shot at as she hung out the washing once, the tea towels were full of holes but luckily she was alright.

Bombing in London was terrible and as we looked towards the city we saw angry red skies and black clouds above, the capital was burning and we had no recourse but to weep for the people, we felt so helpless.

One day my father was home on leave and called for me to come outside, as he had head the soft 'rat-a-tat' of gunfire. An English Spitfire and German Fighter were engaged in a dog fight. Verey flares were fired to light the scene and we craned our heads to look at the fight. It was as clear as daylight.

The two planes swooped down on each other like some weird ballet, first one would swoop and fire and then the other, both climbing in turn to swoop again. But after some time one fighter broke away and flew off, then the other. These duels in the air, often deadly, were like those of knights of old on horseback but instead in aircraft. Often we would hear the planes before we saw them, as they flew high above the clouds, there was only the noise of the engines and sometimes distant gunfire.

5 THE AMERICANS AND
THE GERMANS

To understand how we felt about the American soldiers, we should have lived amongst them. Many people did not like them, but we must not forget that without them we would have lost the war, as our situation was desperate. Churchill kept asking for them to help us but received a negative response, then at the eleventh hour they came in and poured into our country in their thousands.

The Americans were very brave during the war, many of them sacrificed their lives for us. We loved them, with their loud music and determination to help us, we needed that as we felt so alone at the time. They held parties at Christmas for orphaned children at the children's home and had a Santa Claus. Many Americans were killed in action pushing through Normandy in France.

Sometimes soldiers would run away from their regiments, but not many. One American went on the run from the local camp. I was sat at the bottom of our garden reading when I looked up and saw that we had a visitor, a young American deserter turning over our rubbish heaps in search of food. I went back into the house to tell my sister so she could telephone the Military Police to collect him. They duly turned up and he went quietly.

6 AFTERNOON TEAS

There was a lighter side to life and one of these was afternoon teas, which we children always looked forward to.

It was important to take a ration of sugar and margarine, even slices of bread, as we were all so short of food; these delightful interludes could not take place without them.

One of the places in which I loved to visit was a large house with many rooms. The family that lived there seemed to be vast with grandparents in evidence, grown up children and grandchildren. There were horses to ride and other children who I liked, such as Raymond, a boy the same age as myself, and two other boys.

The grandfather spent a lot of time in a chair as he was practically bedridden. He was a most cultured man and kind, and would play a favourite game of guess which hand the chocolate was in which I loved, as chocolate was so scarce.

One day when we were having tea and had been playing with another grandchild, curly haired Matthew (his mother was a writer of children's books, Merula Salaman), a quiet man appeared in the doorway. His very presence was magnetic, it was Sir Alec Guinness, who was Matthew's father. The blue eyes were like two beams in a pale face and he gave me a shy smile.

The other boys in the household insisted we go and look

at a goat giving birth which we did and found it fascinating. One boy went on to train as an obstetrician and the other a doctor, so the interest was there.

We loved the house and in one room there was even a cubbyhole where we could view people moving below! I hasten to add, that we are only ever saw a young woman unpacking, nothing exciting.

7 ENTERTAINMENT AND
THE SEASONS

Although there was no television, we had our radio as I have mentioned. It was a large magnificent set which ran off batteries and had a lovely sound. Obviously we listened to Children's Hour, but also ITMA hosted by Tommy Handley. 'Music whilst you work' was mainly for people working in the munitions factories, but we loved it.

Mother always liked the "Man in Black" thriller stories, which she listened to in her sitting room, it was far too frightening for us. One day I crept down from my bed and sat on the stairs outside her room to hear it, I was terrified. I had the most scary nightmares that night, guess that it served me right!

We had The Telegraph and The Daily Mirror newspapers delivered to us, but if there was something in them which we would find upsetting we were banned from reading it. Daddy particularly liked the comic strip featuring Jane and her little dog.

Whilst Daddy was in Blackpool, there was of course no lighting of the famous Golden Mile. Shows though still went on to keep the forces entertained. He once attended a show with a revolving dais and men and women that were covered in gold went slowly around. He said that it looked really beautiful. He also adored Mae West and once brought home some ashtrays with pin ups on them, much to my mother's disgust!

About once a month we had the village dance. This was held in the village hall and was a great event, everybody would eagerly partake and it helped keep the community together. Wearing the best dress we could afford from our coupon allowance, our hair neatly curled, we danced around to gramophone music (often Victor Sylvester as we had been learning to dance from his radio lessons) participating in the Waltz, Foxtrot and Quick Step (I remember dancing with father whilst wearing a bright yellow parachute nylon nightdress with puff sleeves, one evening at home. I felt very grown up) As there was often a shortage of boys we would usually dance with other girls or women, most of whom had been left behind by their men who had gone to war. What boys remained were shy and sat awkwardly in a row facing the girls. Wearing high heels that were often too tight, we would whirl the night away. Cups of tea and lemonade on a fold-up table were the only refreshments available as the gramophone music played on. The boys wore Brylcreem in their hair to tame it. There was also the ladies' "Excuse Me" dance, where us girls could ask the boys to dance (especially good for boys who were too shy to ask) or cut in with someone we liked whom was already dancing with another.

One evening there was magic in the air and a feeling of excitement as I had heard that there were some new people in the village. A handsome man, dressed in ballroom attire, swept me up in his arms and into a beautiful waltz. I felt like I was floating on air and my feet were liquid, I was so enthralled! After he took me back to my seat and I sadly did not see him again. Of course the war was often like that, people would come and go and you would not ask them probing questions or gossip. At the end of the night it would be a lovely walk home through a scented country lane and in spring there was always the strong smell of lilac.

We certainly weren't short of entertainment too, as well as the village hall dances, we went to the local picture house in Midhurst and watched some good films. Some of the American films had beautiful kitchens. All the courting couples sat at the back, I don't think that they saw much of the films! We saw Pathe News and that was the first time I saw pictures from German death camps, I could not believe it and thought it was from another world and untrue. I couldn't envisage that humans could do such obscene acts to others, as my mother said "Man's inhumanity to man."

If there wasn't a bus, we had to trek three miles there and back with a torch. We didn't mind as we were used to walking everywhere and it was mainly safe, my brother would occasionally thumb us lifts.

I always looked forward to various seasonal activities, such as Easter and Halloween. For the former, Mother would always make up beautiful, colourful bouquets of primroses and violets, often to take to our daily keep, Mrs. Wakeford. For Halloween, we would decorate an old outbuilding with lots of colourful autumnal leaves and light lamps and then competitively bob for red apples! I remember the smell from the candles that burned in the hollowed out turnips, simply putrid! We ate ginger biscuits and cooked sausages whilst drinking lemonade. Mother was very superstitious and fixed a scythe over the kitchen door to cut any witch that entered's head off. This was the night that allegedly all the souls and evil spirits were loose, but we loved Halloween. Then it was off to bed with our cocoa and to pull the blankets over our heads to hide from any prowling witches!

Christmas was another lovely time, but I do not remember my father being there much. We had a chicken if we were lucky, with bread sauce and Bisto, swede, parsnips, roast potatoes and brussel sprouts, followed by Christmas pudding (homemade of course using a wartime recipe).

Mother made a cake and the decorations came out every year, with lighted candles on the tree. We wore lovely, elaborate hats (I wonder what happened to them?) and crafted our own decorations out of paper strips and red berried holly from outside. I would walk to Midhurst to buy a Christmas tree (only a medium-sized one) which I would carry home, the dye from my green wedge shoes leaving a little coloured trail in the snow. As I walked across the fields I hoped no cows were lying asleep, as once I had unfortunately landed on one (I did not have a torch, we only had one kept at the house as we didn't have many batteries). We were used to finding our way around the farm in the dark and sometimes our dog Laddie would guide us, as he knew every path and obstacle.

We didn't have many presents as there were no toyshops or presents in the shops. Mother sent for a book or doll when I was younger from Barkers of Kensington or Porters. We all had stockings though, filled with chocolate coins, fruit and a pack of cards or a joke.

Usually on Christmas Day after tea, we would perform a Christmas play, written by my elder sisters. It was however more of a pantomime! I was once a Roman Soldier and a fairy in a Midsummer Night's Dream, for the latter I wore a lovely pink fairy dress, but unfortunately my combinations fell down as I had not taken them off! I also played Dick Whittington's cat and was made to wear an elaborate catsuit made out of black crepe paper. Unfortunately (and inevitably) it split when I was on all fours playing said creature, so rather embarrassingly I made a hasty retreat! Of course my parents always enjoyed these plays, especially Daddy, when he was rarely at home.

When the snow was on the ground, everything felt hushed like a silent fairy tale and only the tracks of the rabbits and birds made little trails in the snow. Once the whole of our water supply froze up and we had no water for the cattle or to make tea, so the local fire brigade turned up with churns of water for us and the cattle, who had crowded around the fireman as they broke the ice and poured in the water, the breath of the animals filled the air with puffs of cloud. We would of course, enjoy sledging. The best sledges were ones made with corrugated iron sheets and tin trays – although sometimes dangerous as one once accidently hit me and cut my head! The local youths would have snowball fights but unfortunately would often put stones in them, very nasty! If the pond on the Common froze over we would pull each other over the ice in an old tin bath which was very exciting, especially the speeds we reached. I loved to walk in the woods with Laddie making tracks in the fresh snow, Laddie chasing a rabbit or pheasant. (After the war, Benbow Pond on the Cowdray Estate was frozen over and several cars round the edge had their headlights on the ice, while people skated.)

There was also the village fete that was held in the Guinness family's house garden! The two legged race and sack race were eagerly participated in by all, but I was useless at sports and felt hopeless. However the lemonade and cake that we consumed after made up for it. You could also bowl for a pig which would be won by a lucky person and taken home to fatten up.

8 THE GYPSIES

During a late summer, the gypsies came to Sussex. I noticed them first as I came home from school, camped on the farm track leading up to Snapelands. I went round and used the main track but all day they were on my mind. As the evening came and dusk fell, my curiosity got the better of me and I slipped through the fields to hide behind the gatepost to peer at them. I knew them well, fine women with brown eyes and silver earrings. The brightly coloured red, green and gold caravan was attached to a rough, black horse eating and tethered to the bushes.

The dark-haired gypsies sat around the fire – their can of food boiling over and blackened smoke drifting up, the smell of burning wood. There didn't seem to be any children in the camp. The man who was sitting there noticed me, his eyes were wild and watchful, unfettered by a complicated life. He wore an old tweed coat and a brown hat and we stared at each other inquisitively.

What an exciting life, they led, the freedom of the road and constant movement. I felt like going too, but if I did, I may not have been seen again. My mother had warned me that the gypsies liked fair-haired children and would often take them away. The thought of never seeing my family again made me run back to the safety of the farmhouse.

Still I could hear their voices, I hoped that they did not

decide to follow me. I lay awake thinking of them in their snug caravan, the embers of their fire dying.

The next day I went back to where they had stayed but they had long gone. There was no mess, no disgarded rags or tins, only a neatly flattened fire patch, the true Romany leaves no mess.

It was possible then to get beautifully made pegs of white wood created by the gypsies, they lasted for years. Sometimes a gypsy woman came to the door with a basket of white heather. Lucky heather they called it, but I never found it so. They would expect to be paid in coins, the palm crossed. Once unable to get to a stall at a jumble sale, a gypsy woman had pushed a way forward for me. One poor gypsy on leaving the pub had some boys steal £500 from his pockets. Sometimes we would see one come by with his horse, the hoarse cry of 'Rag and Bone' as they came to collect old fridges and furniture. 'The Travellers' we called them, soon to disappear as silently as they had appeared, leading their nomadic lifestyle. Now so much of our countryside has disappeared and many have now got houses and settled. Their way of life is rapidly dying, almost like an endangered species.

I remember in one part of North Hampshire, a gypsy encampment at the end of a lady's garden. She had gone away on holiday leaving no door locked and had come back to an untouched home.

Later that year we had another visitor, a tramp who came to the house for a meal. My mother had a special plate that she kept for him and a chair. She would give him a meal and a warm coat. He would leave a sign for any other tramps to let them know that they would receive food or clothes if they knocked on the door. So there was a lot of activity at our place!

They are proud people whom should be allowed to continue their lives in peace.

9 DAY TO DAY LIVING

It may seem strange, but looking back now, it seems as if there was more security then than now. Life went on day to day. Everyone tried their best in strained circumstances to keep going in as normal a way as possible. We would cover our windows with grey blankets to hide any chinks of light as it was deemed too risky to have much light at night of course.

Crime was very low, we never locked our doors except at night or needed burglar alarms and women, elderly and children could all walk freely about in the evening. The men of the village would take on any rogue, some justice being handed out to a wife beater. Although, whilst father was away we did feel unprotected and vulnerable. Child molestation was almost unheard of. We were only told to be careful of soldiers. The only fear was from dogs allowed to roam. Nowadays the fear is still there, but of people not the war.

Social life went on as normal, the village shop regularly opened and closed, the butcher delivered the meat rations (sometimes a nice joint) bought with all our coupons. The bread was left in our breadbox at the top of the lane, fresh and white for tea with a scraping of margarine and jam.

There were still a lot of men working on the farms (who were exempt from duty) and other male figures such as the local vicar, so we were not living in a wholly female society and it was a good balance.

We lived in fear of invasion and everything would stop for the news, woe betide anyone who spoke during this! At night we would all gather around the radio.

It seemed very important to keep some order in our lives because we felt more in charge and therefore timetables were rigid. Sometimes it felt like it would always be like this, the farm life with the countryside unrolling around us each day and the never ending seasons.

In the hall of the farmhouse my father's double-barrelled shotgun hung on the wall, the cartridges stashed in a drawer. We had been given strict instructions to use it if any German tried to enter the house. We had discussed what would happen to us in an invasion. "It might be better if you took aspirin", my father said, as we women would all be sent to the camps to be used for further breeding by the Germans. We accepted this as normal and it did not preoccupy too much of our thoughts as there was so much else to do.

I always felt paranoid that I might be snatched by a German on my way home from school through the cornfields. My only instinct if that did happen would be to run like hell until I reached the safety of home.

10 A SUSSEX CHILDHOOD

It always seemed like summer during the Second World War in our village, As I wandered down the street houses were clustered together and I could smell warm brick, scents of summer on the breeze, lilies, roses and other non-definable flora and fauna. Mother had sent me to the shoemakers to get the buckle sewn on my sandal, so I carried them in my hand and walked barefoot on the hot, tarmac road.

When I arrived at the shoemaker's house, the cool darkness of his home was a welcome relief. The shoemaker sat squarely on his chair, my tiny sandal held in his rough hand and pressed it into the leather apron he wore, which gave off the evocative smell of new shoes. We exchanged greetings and spoke little as he deftly sewed my buckle back on. He was surrounded by piles of shoes also waiting to be mended – rough boots, ladies' dainty heels, all piled on the brickwork of the floor.

The task finished, I promptly paid him and now fully shod wondered if I should wander back home to the old farmhouse or wander to the fields and nearby river. The enticing smell of wild garlic from its banks, the colourful flash of a kingfisher's wing and interesting small fish glimpsed in the shallows were a temptation. Sometimes the elvers swarmed on their return to the sea, white bodies with clinging mouths and wraithlike forms. Once I had caught them and put them in a jar, their small mouths pressed against the glass, but they had frightened me so I had swiftly put them back in the water. I would often explore the river, sliding down the wet bank. But I decided to return home, the thought of tea (the milk from which came in a churn straight from our cows milked that very afternoon), bread and jam, fish paste and cake made with dried egg was very agreeable.

11 AND A NIGHTINGALE SANG

At Snapelands we were surrounded by the most beautiful woods and land, which went on for miles. Our garden had a small copse and paddock running into each other at the back. Much wildlife inhabited the woods – foxes, weasels and stoats etc.

The nightingales were numerous and also the nightjar. The nightingale was a brown, shy bird, seldom seen but often heard in Sussex. I have heard it in other places too.

My mother suggested one warm evening that we go and listen to this wonderful bird and so we made our way to the clearing in the copse. The moonlight had an unearthly glow and soon we heard the clear and familiar notes, one silver peal after another, the most wonderful sound.

I reflected that the world was in chaos but here was a bird singing away as if there were no bombs, displaced people or broken homes. It made me feel that nature had the answer to all this disruption and that we should try and keep ourselves free of war as the nightingale had. It calmed my mind. There were many such moments in the war when our souls were drawn together and briefly uplifted.

We had a lot of freedom in the country despite the war and the constant fear of attacks.

12 SCHOOL

When I turned seven I attended school as that was the expected age to start your education. Miss Osbourne's private school was in an old artist's studio, who had hanged himself from the stair rail. Stairs were built at the end of the room, going past a huge picture window, which gave light to the studio. One day she claimed that she had heard a voice call her name 'Dorothy' but there was nobody there, spooky! However, I was often alone in the studio and did not feel at all afraid.

My sisters Elaine, Gay, Diana, brother Gregory and I attended the school which we walked to every day along the narrow lanes for over a mile at least and with no pavements, so that one had to scramble up the side of the banks if traffic came by (which was rarely as petrol was strictly rationed - mainly to farmers with a tractor or for transportation for cattle, but some people were allowed small rations for shopping etc.)

Miss Osbourne was that rare person, a wonderful creative teacher, and I feel privileged to have known her. She made all learning a great adventure, a rare quality even nowadays.

We were taught to read and learn the alphabet using a blackboard with the words written out on it, when we had learned each word we were called up to the teacher and had to read the word out to the class. I remember standing by Miss Osbourne and reading out 'Cat' and feeling a great sense of achievement! I couldn't wait to learn more words and it was then that my great love for reading began. I also learned all my times tables and loved History. I won the term prize and got a book and gold star. At age thirteen I was reading War and Peace.

We also would knit scarves for the sailors out at sea and sang the hymn, "For Those In Peril On The Sea."

Our school dinners were shocking – terrible stews and grey rice pudding (in which once I found a slug!), tasteless and stringy cabbage, the list goes on! I wore black school knickers with pockets so sometimes I would put some of the unappealing food in them and then throw it down the toilet when I got the chance at break time!

We played games in the garden such as rounders or cricket. But on one unfortunate occasion I was thrown face down in the manure heap at the bottom by the badly behaved boys when I went out to play.

Once a German bomber blew out the studio window causing mayhem with our nerves, especially for some of the London evacuees.

Although I was very happy here despite this, all was to come to an end when Miss Osbourne fell ill with cancer of the stomach and had to leave for treatment so consequently sold the school (she did recover but did not return to her profession). Teaching was resumed by another teacher in the village hall but I began to suffer with my nerves. I had a breakdown due to the stressful events of the war and could not stop crying. Matters came to a head when an army unit became active nearby and started storing their ammunition in a cupboard at the hall, Tommies would barge in and out at all times of the day carrying it.

Mother took me to the doctor and he suggested I stayed at home for a year to recover. This meant I could help out on the farm and be with my mother but my schoolwork suffered as result. Gregory said that he thought I had gone mad and I think I had! Children's nerves are wrecked by wars. Only men like wars!

Despite the fact that I did not attend school for several years after, I do not consider that I have missed out on learning at all and in later life attended Art and Open University courses. What teaching we did have then was good considering the war, which had disrupted everything.

13 NATURE WALKS

One of the greatest delights at school was to be taken on a nature walk. Shortly after arriving at school, we would be told that we were going on a walk. I think that these are so important to schools as you learn to appreciate nature and realise its place in your life and how much it plays an integral part.

The early spring walks were the best, the anticipation of the new season, the fresh clean air and the busy river bubbling away. We were allowed to pick pussy willows and primroses (it was so nice to be able to take these home and put them in a jam jar on the farmhouse window sill). Excited birds called to each other and the earth was awakening again. The sticky horse chestnut bud bursting open gave me great satisfaction. There seemed to be so much more to learn on one of these expeditions than being cooped up in a classroom.

14 MY FATHER AND HERITAGE

Like so many, all the men in my family were at war. My mother's brother Edgar was at the war office and his bathroom was blown up, luckily missing him, he was engaged in secret war work. He was at the underground and played chess games on air, each move a code to give information for the resistance.

My Uncle Edmund (my father's sister's husband) escaped from Austria and Germany, he was Jewish and running for his life. He built a successful business in Coventry and went on to work in the Secret Service at the BBC.

My father was a veteran of WW1. He had gone over the top at the Somme and then was responsible for organising stretcher-bearers under fire on the battlefield and bringing out the wounded. He should have got a medal for his bravery one soldier said.

Father was born in Plymouth in 1896 and had three sisters. His father also had a dental practice. Father attended Plymouth Grammar School and at the age of eighteen, when WW1 had broken out, he went with his friends to do Officers' Training at Sandhurst. He took his sword and went into battle, seeing his many friends that he had grown up with killed in battle, their heads blown or cut off. Riding on horseback and all around you your friends dying must have been so dreadful to even envisage, especially when a few weeks before you had been fighting in mock-battles in the streets of Plymouth. You grew up quickly then, no teenage years for you. Young, then suddenly old as you stared death in the face and if you were lucky to survive, only to fight again.

My father was a good man, I never heard him grumble. He brought me up without a fuss, he taught me to paint a chair and be capable, but most importantly to respect myself as well others. To remember that I was an officer's daughter, always;

"Goodnight Daddy, you are buried in your uniform, a soldier to the end. You took us on lovely picnics when you were on leave, we made tea on a smoky kettle over a fire and you taught me to fish, and even to march!"

My father's family was most interesting, a mixture of good and bad, poet, peasant and aristocrat. Anglo-Irish, they had originated from Cork in Ireland where my ancestor Earl Fowler took ship and fled to Cornwall when they had burned down his house. Landing on the shore was the Earl, his wife, their servant and their baby son, whom I am descended from. They started a long line of noble Fowlers, married into the Fry family – Patricia, sister of Elizabeth, and were farmers at Ilfracombe in Devon. For two hundred years they were based in Devon, my great grandfather William was Captain of his own ship (sailing from Plymouth) and his diary is in Plymouth Museum. Once he went back to visit Ilfracombe and the villagers were very surprised to see him in his Captain's uniform!

One Fowler was an aide to Wolsey and was at Henry V111s court, marrying Catherine of Aragon's sister. He survived the court.

Vicars, bishops, soldiers, sailors, medical men and gardeners are also present in the family tree. Research indicates Viking descent also, so we are an unusual family.

Villagers used to say that the Fowler's "Were not of this world!". There are links with the Royal Family in the household of past centuries and blood links with John the Gallant and Bonnie Prince Charles. Old documents show a relative, Richard Fowler, fought for Richard 1st on the battlefield, rushing up and down on his white horse with his musket, the King was very pleased. The Fowlers were also rich landowners based in Lincolnshire and Northamptonshire, where they had a large mansion, but due to high taxes lost their money. Now the money comes back to them via computers and American connections. We should be pleased whatever our roots are, as it shows that we all have a history and that is our future. Past relatives' genes are imprinted on us. I love gardening and I had an ancestor who was a Head Gardener. I often go into our garden and know just where to place a plant or how it should be trained, I know a lot I could not have possibly learned.

It's 2001 as I write this and my family is growing, with several relatives marrying around the world. We are a very cosmopolitan family!

15 MEN DURING THE WAR

Men weren't exactly on short supply during the war, there were many about but not available to me as I was a skinny girl and far too young! I envied my older sisters, one a V.A.D. at a naval hospital and the other at a NAAFI in Tangmere.

Boyfriends seemed quite intimidating to my sisters and I at this time. My parents would insist that we were all home and indoors by 10pm and if we weren't we found ourselves in a lot of trouble. My father kept a large, black walking stick in the hall and Mother would prowl the village looking for her daughters! We all lived in fear of that wobbly, black stick! In those days disciplining one's children was a responsibility parents took seriously. Politeness was expected and consideration to one's elders mandatory. A boy was expected to lift or touch his cap when passing a lady he knew in the street. I did not have a serious boyfriend until my late twenties, so strong was the discipline that was instilled in me.

We now virtually did not have a father as he was obviously away, destination unknown, and very seldom came home at all. He did say once that he had been blown down the stairs at Blackpool Tower by bombs but we were not to gossip about anything we heard or saw of course. Ironically, despite the 'Loose lips sink ships' mantra, the grapevine was uncommonly good and often word of mouth was more factual than the news.

It was difficult to adapt to a man's presence in the house and Gregory had got a bit out of hand so immediately started playing my father up when he was at home by locking my poor father in the hen house! When of course he came after Gregory shouting, Gregory immediately ran to hide in the woods and didn't come back until dark. Mother tried to discipline him but he was a really naughty boy and ran away from home, the police found him and brought him back. After this, he was sent to a private boarding school in Billingshurst but ran away again after some other boys tried to put his head down the toilet and do other horrible things. So I do think that it is very necessary to have a permanent male presence in the home.

Apart from my father, there were other men that were around during WW2. Our gardener, Mr. Nicholls, who had worked in Canada, had white hair, which he claimed was caused by a bear attack. He planted and grew all our vegetables so we always had a fresh supply of them, and even rescued me from a tree once that I had climbed and couldn't get down from.

Some girls would chase the visiting Yanks for nylons and chocolate and the promise of a better life. They were always polite to women and never surly, some were only seventeen. We called them G.I.s. Many women got married to them and emigrated to the States, but some came back disappointed with their lives there. One girl was introduced to her mother-in-law, who was sitting in a tepee and smoking a pipe. Some G.I.s were married and had wives and families back home, other girls became pregnant and were left on their own with their babies.

In Midhurst, there were many fights between the G.I.s and local lads culminating in arrival of the American Military Police. A lot of jealously raged amongst American and British men then.

We all loved the thumping sounds of the American bands – the music flowed with energy and life. We could listen to Glen Miller playing on the American Forces Network with just the twiddle of the radio knob and a tweak of the aerial. The sounds gave us hope and comfort during the dark days of the war, we felt invincible. It was certainly a welcome change from Vera Lynn's "We'll Meet Again" – although still a very beautiful song.

Later on towards the end of the war, the German P.O.W.s came. Many indoctrinated to such a degree that it was dangerous to deal with them.

My father had the job of caring for the S.S. Officers and had to see their teeth. Whilst he was treating them a Tommy with a machine gun stood by. They were completely taken over by Hitler's terror machine.

After the war a lorry load of the Germans came to work in the fields. One day I was riding my bicycle to the farm and the lorry came by. Whether it was from fear, I don't know, but I fell from my bike and the shopping came out from my basket. From out of the vehicle faces peered, some had faces like nightmares – harsh, gaunt and cruel, but several jumped out and picked me back up. They packed my basket and clicked their heels when they had finished. I was shaking.

We were certainly not allowed to fraternise with them by law as they brought such fear to our lives. One said bitterly to my mother "You tell your children to come indoors when we are around, you think that we are monsters but we are not." Some were very cruel, one tried to kill a dog with a hammer. It ran into our house terrified, we tried to catch it but it ran back out and disappeared.

Other men came into our lives too. The vicar, whom Mother didn't like, told us to let her know if he came along and pretend that she was out.

Once we saw a flying cassock coming down the lane and warned Mother. She ran to the loft with the speed of lightning. "Where's your mother, children?" he enquired benevolently. "Hiding upstairs away from you!." I don't think he called again. There was one boy called Raymond (who liked to catch spiders in matchboxes) that I was very keen on and hoped that he would marry me one day. We went swimming in a huge lake in Ludgershall, but did not realise that there was a swan's nest there. Suddenly this huge swan flew out at us and started attacking us with its large wings, I knew that I could not get away and Raymond turned back to save me, shouting and waving his arms at it to leave me alone.

But the household was matriarchal and we found it difficult to make relationships with men later in life, as they were so intermittent a presence.

When Grandfather visited us the animals all rushed out to greet him, but I longed for a bedtime story from my father. Because he was seldom at home, the gossip in the village speculated that he was really a German spy, when of course he was fighting for our country. So we children would be mercilessly taunted by other village children, but our family learned to fight back and get respect. Of course we did wonder if we were spies! Was Daddy a German spy? A local German lady had also been falsely accused. We all felt very sorry for her, but war is cruel and makes no distinctions.

16 FOOD IN THE WAR

We were lucky living in the country. Although we had ration books and it was sometimes a struggle to save them up, because we were running a farm, we had access to fresh food that perhaps other people did not have. Mother was a very good cook, so she eagerly followed Good Housekeeping, Marguerite Patten and Ministry of Food recipes. We had a great vegetable garden and hens eggs, ducks and milk from the farm. A regular menu was kept to, all our meat rations for a joint on Sunday, really good organic meat too. Shepherds Pie made with the leftovers on Monday, cauliflower cheese, ham and salad, plenty of cake made with dried eggs. Jellies, milk jellies and marvellous wild rabbit stews, I have never had such good ones. We also had bread sausage, made from bread, seasoned and then fried. The local Lord donated venison and a sack of potatoes appeared as if by magic. Mother once tried us out with whale meat that unfortunately tasted like rubber, we hated it, never again! We had various fruit trees – Victoria plums, Beauty of Bath eating apples and Bramley cookers, which mother made into dumplings and crumble. Father once sent a duck in the post. We had one sweet ration we ate in one go! Fry's Chocolate Cream was a favourite and delicious, which we bought from the village store.

The bread was baked locally and was like no other, fresh and wonderful. I always looked forward to retrieving it from our box at the end of the lane.

There were also various social engagements, sometimes at a children's party we would be treated to strawberry ice cream and other culinary delights.

Some families were like The Great Gatsby and a chauffeur would tuck a rug over my legs and the son of the family, as we drove to Midhurst for some shopping. Another time I tried Turkish Delight for the first time, given to me from a famous actor's wife, and chocolate, what a treat! I remember also the beautiful Chinese lanterns, roses and lavenders in the garden. There was certainly some social status difference between various families. Some of their lives seemed hardly changed at all during the war, apart from husbands who were away on service, of which I suspect were V.I.P.s.

One lovely day out having tea with a family, we were taken to see a pig being cured with salt, hanging from an annexe next to the kitchen. Of course many people kept a pig and when it was ready the local policeman would appear as it was killed. I don't know why, it couldn't have been fair play as its throat was cut and the screams were awful. Poor pig. Needless to say we did not keep a pig only hens, which we sold for other people to kill.

I think that we were healthy because food was so natural then, although it was small in portions, it did not have additives and insecticides. I dread to think what is now building up in our bodies. Also there were no petrol fumes so pollution was not as high and everything was very clean, the air very fresh.

I believe that the men of war had all the best food which was only right. We did well though, I never saw an obese or skinny type, so we must have had an adequate diet.

17 THE WOODS AND LAND

We could easily spend all day in beautiful woods and land belonging to Lord Cowdray and Lord L.econfield. The scent of the woods and spring was a smell like no other, a wonderful aroma of primroses, bluebells and other flora, alongside the pussy willows that buzzed to the sound of many bees, the yellow pollen floating away on the wind. The primroses had different shades of yellow, some very pale. White anemones waved their delicate heads in the winds and celandines clustered together like in a Japanese impressionist painting. There were also beautiful wild daffodils but sometimes the gypsies would pick them. I found various exciting places where I could walk amongst the violets that scattered the banks and see the odd adder or lizard. One day the farmer pointed out a nest of baby adders with an adult waving and weaving, looking like Medusa. He told me to be careful as he drew me back' "they will be alright if you don't disturb them," he said. A snake bite could be fatal then as there was no anti-venom. I also saw an owl with its eyes open, I did not know whether it was dead or alive and wandered on straight into a wasp's nest. The angry insects flew up into a raging cloud but I managed to jump through a hedge and luckily they lost track of me. Deer abounded and I had seen a herd in the wood, they stopped at my approach, looked at me with curiosity and then ran swiftly away.

In the woods, the smell of moss, leaves and water was potent and there was the sound of the stream where clear water flowed. Newts could be caught and put in jam jars, but we always put them back. I put my Wellington boots on and lowered myself into the water, in some places it was shallow and others deep. I knew that it would come over the top of my boots and the first tickle of ice cold water shocked me, but soon filled my boots and spilled over the top. Looking down I saw caddis larvae, which had stuck many objects to its shell, straw, small stones etc. Some caddis flies had so much stuck to them that they could only move slowly along the bottom of the stream. They reminded me of people, collecting so many objects that they were weighed down in life.

I was fascinated with the birds, they made nests everywhere, especially in the hedges and around the edge of the pond. I decided to do some mixed breeding and took some eggs from one nest and swopped them over. But the birds took care of the changed babies!

Sometimes I would put out a little ladder from my bedroom window and creep out in my nightdress when I was supposed to be tucked up in bed. I would enjoy running in the fields when it turned dusk and feel the warm to cool evening air. The smell of the lilies and meadowsweet would be intoxicating and I would see the mystical shape of the barn owl flying over my head. Bats flitted high and low, swooping for insects and I would see the odd white rabbit tail dive into the nearest bush in the dim light whilst I ran. I would then creep back to my bed with my feet wet from dew to fall into a happy and contented sleep.

The river Rother flowed through the fields by St. Peters Church and my sisters and brother would often go swimming in the cool waters. Sometimes elvers (baby eels) would swarm down the river and we could catch them but always let them go. Butterflies fluttered by like little coloured flags and large bumble bees bumbled around. We often saw a woodpecker and would pick the chestnuts from the trees to bring them home. I loved the sound of the satisfying pop they made when we warmed them on the open fire to share amongst us.

We would also have picnics with mother at noon on the heather covered Blackdown Hill, where primitive man had made a barrow (one of the first settlements). In summer it was covered in blueberries which I loved picking and delicious wild strawberries, my fingers turning a gradual shade of blue and red.

In the woods was the gamekeeper to Lord Cowdray, Ernie Boxall's cottage. As you approached his home a rather rank smell emanated from the dwelling, which came from the dead creatures hung on the rack outside to dry and frighten predators. Mr. Boxall was a rather bad tempered man, although we loved his black cherries which hung from an enormous tree and tasted divine. Myself and him did not see eye to eye, as I found the wire traps he set for rabbits most cruel. Once I had heard the scream of a young rabbit caught in his trap, I ran to try and free it but saw the gamekeeper coming towards me and just managed to get away in time.

There were lots of beautiful purple rhododendrons in the woods, they grew so thickly in a clump that we could climb over them and walk along the top. My sisters and I shouted with delight as we rolled around, sometimes falling through but luckily not hurting ourselves. When we were playing there we heard a shout, "Stop it!" from Mr. Boxall so fled in terror. I had heard that he had shot himself with a double-barrelled shotgun but I don't know the circumstances. Although he did not care for us he got on well with my father and he would visit him often when he was on leave. We were pretty wild at times and definitely needed a more frequent male presence.

I would often and albeit rather reluctantly, join the

pheasant shooting at Lord Cowdray's Estate. On a cold winter's morning, my mother and I along with some local boys and men would bang and shout to startle the pheasants and get them to fly up. The loud noise of guns and dogs howling left me cold and I did not get asked again.

I have never been one for killing although my father was into fishing and shooting. I certainly do not believe that we should kill anything unless there is a good reason. I think that we do need a certain amount of protein i.e. eggs, fish and meat in moderation but killing for sport, no. We have to make our own minds up and not be pressurised into anything because everybody else does it.

Despite the war the woods remained coppiced and well maintained with the smell of woodsmoke and the sound of wood chopping.

Now some of the woods are privately owned but you can still get hazel nuts in the autumn.

18 THE VILLAGERS

Because we attended a small private school we were thought of as snobs. I didn't mind - I was proud to be an Officer's daughter and that my father was fighting for Britain. I was small for my age and sometimes would come home alone. One day as I approached the farm track about eight village children crept out from where they had been hiding to beat me up. One of them suddenly came at me with a sack of apples and started to hit me then took my bike away. By this point I had really had enough so grabbed my assailant and threw him to the ground. I grabbed his head and banged it on the road repeatedly! "Get off, she's hitting me!" he screamed. The two larger boys of the group gently removed me from my attacker, dusted me down and gave me my treasured bike back. From then on they never touched me again as they knew that I was able to stand my ground.

My mother was very shy and also suddenly had to deal with people in my father's absence. But she coped well and even went alone to visit a notoriously difficult family, becoming firm friends with the female members of the group.

When you live in towns you have a very fluid, cosmopolitan approach to life, but of course villages are a far different affair. I have since met some of the people that

I grew up with and who have remained in the same village, although some have left for different employment and a change.

19 A TRUE ENGLISH VILLAGE

Most of our laundry we did ourselves, but some would go to the village to be taken in by woman who laundered in her back room at her cottage, who when answering the door would appear in a cloud of steam! There was a washroom with lines hanging from the ceiling and damp clothes pegged on them, an assortment of long johns, bloomers and all manner of garments. The boiling water was kept hot by the fire under the boiler and the smell of washing soap was heavy on the air. I was sent to collect a brown paper parcel of clean clothes (my sister usually collected it) that had been neatly folded and ironed. But I was afraid to go as the lady had a grown-up son who was mentally disabled and who used to chase me. She would always tell me that it was alright and not to be afraid, even though I still was.

Many of these cottages had wells and all water had to be drawn from them, sometimes there would be one well for several cottages. I would often peer down them and they were always covered with a wooden lid to keep the water clean and safeguard the chicken.

During the warmer months our grey blankets were washed which was always a job for the children. The white bath was filled with warm water and soap flakes were poured in. We would then jump in with bare feet and tread the cloth, the suds squeezed between our toes. Then the blankets would be rinsed and hung out to dry.

Then there would be a trip to the thriving blacksmiths, I would go with June and take our big carthorse. I usually ended up holding the horse's head but this particular blacksmith was wonderful with horses so there was no need. The forge glowed red and with expert hands the smithy measured the horses foot and deftly took the shoe from the hot coals, shaping it to the correct size. Then with a 'whoosh' sound he put the shoe in cold water and his brown, muscley arms gently pulled the hoof up then tapped the shoe in place, filing and shaping it as he went. It was a great sight to behold and watch such a skilled craftsman at work.

It's hard to know whether Lodsworth made these skilled people or they made Lodsworth, but it was a lovely harmonious village. A good society that was pitted against our enemy, Hitler. Time stood still then, capturing the seven years of war, like a shutter on a camera, and fixing the experience in my mind forever.

20 CHRISTMAS (THE TERRIER)

Opposite the Post Office there was a little green with a huge chestnut tree and a pub called "The Hollist Arms."

When my father was on leave, he would take me with him on Sunday morning and ask the publican if I could come in for lemonade. Usually I would be allowed if they weren't busy and would sit with my father whilst he drank his beer, before we returned for Sunday lunch.

It was on one of these trips alone that my father collected a white terrier puppy and brought it home inside his coat. My mother was delighted when she caught sight of the dog as it was Christmas, so the little terrier was named after the festive season. Christmas was a feisty little girl and had a quick nip if annoyed but she was a good ratter, killing several at once with a bite to the neck. Pure white are not often seen now and I believe they are bred in Germany.

Unfortunately our keeper was always putting down cyanide and Christmas was sadly poisoned. Several cats and another dog also went missing. Many keepers at the time used far too much as they were afraid the pheasant chicks would be lost.

21 BEAUTY AND FASHION

We didn't have many beauty products but my sisters and I were very inventive. We used mudpacks for our skin and iodine to tint our legs (June liked to do this!), with a black pencil to make pretend stocking seams at the back of them. We boiled rain water to wash our hair and skin and used rosemary herbs diluted with gin to give our hair shine as well as chamomile flowers from the chemist for fair hair. Nivea was our face cream, and Potter and Moore's face powder and Ponds vanishing and cold cream. We brushed our hair a lot, a hundred times a day! For our weekly bath we would use Radox in our old tin bath in front of the fire, with water heated on our range. I was having a bath one night when my sister came in with her boyfriend by accident, swiftly followed by hurried retreats all round! Toothpaste was in short supply, so we had toothpowder called Eucryl, a pale pink or Euthymol toothpaste. Gay found out that the gypsies used a silver leafed plant to clean their teeth, so we tried it and it was very effective. We used cream to remove the hairs from our legs.

There were only two perfumes then, Californian Poppy or Violets, not much of choice! In America my Aunty Sybil from New York had Chanel No. 5, what a contrast! Sometimes she would send us trunks of clothes and lacy nylons from our cousin, Jean. We could get some lovely, nice soaps if we were lucky. Wallflower was gorgeous and smelt just like it, and Lux, which was equally as pleasant.

I loved the scented notepaper of which there were several kinds, I particularly favoured gardenia, which was cream coloured with a gardenia pattern. You could use it when you wrote to your family or current beau and it was always nice to receive a scented letter. Very elegant!

Clothes were basic, we had dresses that went below the knee in a pretty print with a belt, they showed off your legs and were very feminine. I wore wedge shoes, blue Wolsey twin sets in blue and tweed shirts brought from Midhurst with my clothes coupons. When I went away I had a smart green velvet hat with a feather, held on with a hatpin and wore gloves. I also occasionally donned a beret.

Underwear was a bit of disaster though, nylon parachute material knickers were uncomfortable but my mother did manage to get a bra for me.

We all wore the same shade of red lipstick, which we weren't really allowed to, but as soon as we were out of the house we would apply it. Sometimes we also had nail varnish.

We were careful with deportment, putting books on our heads and walking around the room. How we sat was important, not too much leg should be shown. I would usually have long hair, secured in the front in a Veronica Lake style, so we were ready for that special man to come into our lives.

Gay rode a white horse through the village just wearing a bikini and caused quite a stir. She also walked up the stairs backwards with a mirror whilst looking in it saying that she would see the face of her one true love in it! Although he never did materialise in the reflection! We also put charms under our pillows as we thought we would dream of 'the one' that night. I think relationships between men and women were much kinder then.

22 SHELTER AND THE AIR RAIDS

Most raids would take place at night, Cynthia would wrap me in a blanket and take me to the air raid shelter which was in the vegetable garden.

Mr. Nicholls had dug the shelter for us. In it we had a bunk bed and chairs, some sweets, a torch and a board game. Unfortunately as it had been built on clay soil, it often filled up with water - which would rise to about a foot and then have to be bailed out with buckets!

Sometimes the Air Raid Warden would ride his bike up and down the street whilst ringing his bell and shouting 'Take cover! Take cover!' – especially to the children whom would be playing some fascinating game and not taking any notice. When the air raid siren went off we would dive under our desks if we were at school or under the kitchen table if there was no time to get to the shelter.

23 D DAY AND OUR VILLAGE/THE BUILD UP TO THE BRITISH INVASION

At the end of May and beginning of June, 1944, we became very aware of the movements of large troops and tanks as well as planes flying overheard during the invasion of our forces on the way to France. At night the persistent drone of them was heard until dawn. It was a comforting sound, troop carriers, gliders, Lancaster Bombers and Spitfires. But nothing flew during daylight hours as it would be too easily spotted. Our little village came to life with all the activity. At this time all the adults had their fingers crossed and were praying. Unfortunately with the build up of the troops, Sussex was not the safe haven we had hoped for. Once, I met a huge group of French Canadians running in the woods who were in training for the invasion.

Meanwhile, Portsmouth, Southampton and the Isle of Wight suffered a terrible battering. Cowes Harbour was bombed and the Radar Station on Bonchurch Downs took a knock, but was soon back in action after a short while!

On another occasion, the noise of bagpipes was heard and my mother and sisters ran up the farm track and saw Mad Jack, a famous green kilted Canadian piper at the head of his men, many hundreds marching in quick time on the dusty road. We all swung on the gate and watched.

The sound of tanks announced the arrival of the British tank regiment, with the white invasion star emblazoned on the front of the vehicles. They were parked on the common and it was a hot summer's day as I remember the strong smell of warm gorse.

One tank crew invited my mother and I to have tea with them, they were cheerful and kind. We gathered around a fire and drank smoky tea from their shared billycan in which a few flies fell and were flicked out by the men.

They lifted us into a tank and we sat inside, it was very cramped and had only a small slit to gaze out from, I don't know how they coped with such a tiny space. Our feet stood on an old carpet or blanket, which was on the steel floor. I often wonder what happened to those men after we had said goodbye and whether any of them came back home from the invasion.

My brother Gregory became very friendly with the C.O. of the American tank regiment. Gregory said that our mother had told the C.O. the tank crew were welcome to sleep on our farm. In the middle of the night a dreadful noise was heard, it was the entire battalion, which had decamped in our farmyard and onto our lawn! Unfortunately the lawn was ruined and they had cut up all our corn bundles to sleep on. The next day June got up to the milk the cows and was horrified at the mess the troops had made! Of course they all heard her and how angry she was, so beat a hasty retreat! Hell hath no fury like my sister! Later the C.O. came back with a bunch of wild flowers and apologised profusely to her.

Later I went down our lane and followed the tank tracks. I could not believe they had left pieces of fruitcake and covered it in condensed milk, such a waste, especially as we were on rations!

When victory was announced on the radio, people who were out working or not listening did not know. I got on my little bike and rode around the village telling everyone. We did not have big celebrations or street parties; it was a very subdued affair. I think that also we were all very tired from the constant years of struggle and worry.

Every time in early June when I smell the familiar smell of hot gorse I am often reminded of the men that bravely fought in the war and I always feel tinged with sadness at the ones that did not return.

24 SAD TIMES AND THE SUMMER OF 1945

When the war ended in 1945 in many ways it came as a great relief, but we were so tired that when Mother heard on the announcement on the radio it was an anti-climax. For so long we had hoped and prayed and worked right up to the very end that we just felt numb. I got on my bike and rode around the village shouting that the, they looked grim and sad.

The 'let down' feeling after the war was tangible, everything seemed grey, indeed grey seemed a favourite colour.

We still had rationing (with the exception of bread) and the men were still away as they had to be demobbed, there was no work to come back to, all their businesses had gone and for many their marriages too.

Now the men started to be nasty to each other as they realised what they had returned to. My father had stored all his dental equipment but when he went to retrieve it, it had gone rusty and was virtually useless. Because of this, he decided to remain in the regular army and ran two dental units in Northern Ireland, where he was stationed. I was 13 and a half at this time and was attending a governess's school in preparation to attend Chichester High School. But at about this time my mother suddenly became ill. She had just given birth to her last child, my baby brother Eric Richard (his second name was the same as the local hospitals), but he was very weak and had a twisted intestine so couldn't keep his milk down. His doctor suggested giving Eric brandy so Mother decided to see another medial professional. Dr. Lush came and said that Eric was near death and must go straight to hospital, so Mother and I took a taxi and rushed through the country lanes to St. Richards Hospital in Chichester. Once there he was operated on immediately and christened by the priest. Luckily he recovered but remained frail and my mother's health began to wane, having so many children and the strain of the war had begun to take its toll. Eventually she was diagnosed with breast cancer and had one breast removed as well as some lymph glands. She came home and for one year seemed to be better but it did not last. Sadly my brother Eric had to remain in a children's home as there was no one to care for him.

I continued with the governess who was a dragon and very bad tempered. She had terrible bad breath and would hit me with a ruler and shouted if I found French difficult. Lord Cowdray attended school with me and sometimes I would get a lift in the family's pony and trap to Easebourne where I studied. Mayor Hollist came back from the army and gave us notice to quit the farm. We were in a terrible state, with mother ill and nowhere to go. June went to see Mr. Budger one of the farmers in the village and he offered us a little cottage called "Woolhurst," with an outside toilet so we took it. It was not really what we were used to but it had to do. I shared a bed with three of my sisters and a mouse ran over my face one night! Gay, Felicity and I were the only girls left and my brother Gregory was in a separate bedroom, where he insisted on keeping his pet ferrets.

Alas there was more trouble to come – I came down with a terrible case of whooping cough and had to sleep downstairs in the scullery, so I could open the window as I couldn't breathe. Mother began to get ill and started to be sick, from then on she stayed in bed and was very weak. My darling sister Diana who was a student nurse came home to care for her. Mother could keep very little down and was eventually moved to Midhurst Cottage Hospital, a private organization.

My poor father was left distraught, he had hoped to provide us with a home in Ireland, Officers' Quarters, now that dream of being together as a family was no more. I used to visit Mother when I left school at Easebourne, up the long drive surrounded by green lawns and into the little hospital. One afternoon I pushed open the door to her room and in the mirror to my left I saw the reflection of my mother, her jewel like violet eyes seemed to be enormous and luminous.

As I bent down to kiss her, she put her arms around me and hugged me close as if she would never let me go. She asked me if she could have some fizzy lemonade as it was the only thing she could keep down. I gave it to her and said, "But Mummy when you come home, you can have as much as you like." "I shan't be coming home," she said. "Take care of your brother Gregory and don't fight too much and of your sister Felicity. You have to be strong for me." I was utterly stunned, I realised she meant she was going to die, but mothers don't die, they are always there to help you and be there for you. I was also angry, how could she die and leave us? But she looked so ill, tiny and frail, her body covered in blue sores.

Soon after she died, my sister said that Mother had opened her arms and smiled one night then said "Jesus" and passed away. I had no experience of humans dying, having only seen the animals on the farm at the end of their life. To me this was the most terrible thing and changed mine and my sibling's world forever. We were completely rudderless with no mother at the helm. I was only fourteen when she passed away in May, 1948, and I always remember the white May blossoms that bloomed in the hedges. My father had got compassionate leave shortly before she died, he stayed in Midhurst at The Spread Eagle Hotel, but every day he came home for supper and tea. He used to sit by the fire looking terribly sad. When his fortnight's leave was over he had to return to the regiment R.A.M.C. Because of this he was not with her at the end, although he stood alone at her grave and cried.

Mother is buried at Apuldram Church near Dell Quay in Chichester and I think she really would have liked to be at Lodsworth, but I had no part in the decision and was engulfed in my grief. I would never be able to be her friend and enjoy her company as an adult. It is a terrible thing to lose a mother, she above all else cares for you against a cruel and heartless world. My brother, younger sister and myself did not attend the funeral.

It was after this that our lives became very sad. Although we remained in the cottage, Cynthia was getting married and the other sisters were away. Gay went to join the WAAF, June left the NAAFI and went to be a nanny, Patricia and Diana were nursing and Elaine was training to be a Pitmans secretary. Gregory remained on the farm until he decided to emigrate to Australia aged only fifteen, he told me, "With mummy gone there is no reason to stay." I said goodbye to him at Liverpool Street Station, he had an overcoat on and seemed cheerful.

I had a series of jobs, one as a mother's keep in the village (to an officer's family) and a terrible one where I scrubbed floors and long passages whilst kneeling on a bit of sacking (later I suffered with arthritis in this part of my body). I also waitressed in Midhurst on Saturdays.

By the time I had reached fifteen or sixteen, my father and grandfather told me I had to get a proper job. I was sad to leave Lodsworth, where I had played with my brothers and sisters and where so many of my formative years had been spent.

I had to let go of the land I loved and my animals. I had a little white duffle bag and in this I placed what was left of my book collection and a plaster cottage (which represented the home that I wanted and left) and I was not to see Lodsworth for a long time after. For several years I worked in various different places, alone and sometimes treated badly. It was a while before I felt settled again, but life moves on and I had to as well. I am proud of the fact that we ran the farm during the war and helped in the war effort, and we were only a bunch of women! Now it seems like a dream and another world. Life had simply taken a different direction than I had hoped for, that was all.

My father married a year after mother's death and unfortunately all our fears of the wicked stepmother came true, but that is a story for another day.

25 REFLECTION ON THE WARTIME

The air raid sirens that are still used in certain areas for prison escapes now still give me the horrors to this day. That familiar sinking feeling in the stomach and slightly sick feeling, war left many scars (some not so visible) for many people.

Life was not so complex or changeable as it is now and although we were at war, in some ways it felt much more stable than nowadays. We need to take some time and try to steady our lives for a better future and to find our inner contentment.

The strange thing was it wasn't in black and white like the old war films, it was in vivid colours like a film and it was so intense you lived everything to the full. Those seven years were the most intense time of my life and it's always there, you can never forget, that is why I am writing this down also because I never want to see another one and if people can read this they will see any war is wrong, it destroys families and disrupts lives and people are killed who had no chance of life.

We meet Germans now, some have been my friends, but never forget the Nazis had been brainwashed to terrible cruelties and given free reign to allow the darkest part of the human soul to take charge. So we of course feared them during the war, especially girls and women, if they invaded us.

We should not need wars, if we are really civilised, life is and should be sacred, not a drop of blood should be spilt by another. War has no place in our futures, surely we should have moved on by now? We are not primitives.

Any nation who thinks that they are supreme above all poses a threat.

The freedom women have today was not known then, but began during the war when their roles changed from wives to running the home, to turning the earth, making munitions and so on. A mixed blessing in many ways, and I do not mean sexual freedom, but of course women are still weaker physically then men and they forget this in many situations. I, for one, know my place!

As for farming, it is the factory for the farmer, the production of food and a way of earning his living. Farmers do not get too fond of their animals as they know that they must be sacrificed but I think that they had a better life then. Hens roamed free range on the farm and garden, cows all had a name in small herds – Daisy, Rosie, and so on. They were hand milked and treated well, no numbers then. They certainly did not seem as stressed as they do nowadays.

Perhaps in our own rush for progress, we have forgotten to savour life as it should be and we may yet find, we shall return in many ways to our roots. The day may be dying of the large businesses and smaller units coming back. The small farm may make a return – less profits but more happiness, we shall see.

So many pilots lost their lives, some of them only eighteen and they didn't even last a week. Also we must realise that without the Battle of Britain we would have been taken over by Germans, who would have swept throughout the world, even America and that would have been the end of civilisation as we know it and the return to the dark ages. Murder, mayhem and psychos would have ruled.

So we will have to decide in the future not to have wars, maybe people will evolve to become more peaceful, I hope so...

Printed in Great Britain
by Amazon